Barbie™

Kensational!

COLORING

THUNDER BAY
P · R · E · S · S

San Diego, California

Thunder Bay Press
An imprint of Printers Row Publishing Group
9717 Pacific Heights Blvd, San Diego, CA 92121
www.thunderbaybooks.com • mail@thunderbaybooks.com

Printers Row Publishing Group is a division of Readerlink Distribution Services, LLC. Thunder Bay Press is a registered trademark of Readerlink Distribution Services, LLC.

Correspondence regarding the content of this book should be sent to Thunder Bay Press, Editorial Department, at the above address.

Thunder Bay Press
Publisher: Peter Norton
Associate Publisher: Ana Parker
Editorial Director: Diane Cain
Art Director: Charles McStravick
Senior Project Editor: Jessica Matteson
Editor: Julie Chapa
Editorial Assistant: Sarah Hillberg
Designer: Brianna Tong
Cover Design: Erica Skatzes
Production Team: Beno Chan, Mimi Oey

ISBN: 978-1-6672-0804-6

Printed in Dongguan, China
First printing, December 2024. RRD/12/24

29 28 27 26 25 1 2 3 4 5

**He's dreamy.
He's stylish.
He's totally
Kensational!**

Step into the phenomenal world of the one and only Ken!
Barbie's legendary friend has been bringing the fun
since 1961, and after years of being an accessory,
now is his time to shine. Turn the pages and color
your way through his many adventures.
It's Ken's world, and we're all just living in it.
Or so he'd like to believe!

Rays for Days!

Your host with **THE MOST.**

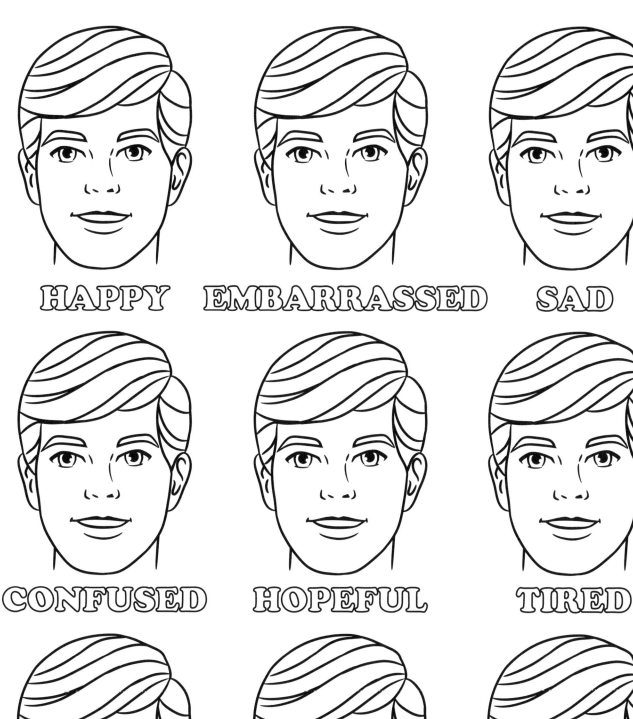

HAPPY EMBARRASSED SAD

CONFUSED HOPEFUL TIRED

GRUMPY EXCITED SURPRISED

Life's a Beach.

KEN YOU DIG IT?

SO MANY FLAKES, SO LITTLE TIME!

POOLSIDE is my BEST SIDE...

Rollin' with my Kentourage.

No pier pressure.

Bringing the
Kentertainment!

Skating through life like...

Let's make a *Racket!*

I can't.

I have a BOARD MEETING.

SHAKE it,
don't
BREAK it.

Take a hike!

Drink in my hand...

toes in the sand.

Things are looking HIP and HUMERUS

Gradu-ATE that!